The **Failure Book**

How 22 **EXTRAORDINARY** People **PERSISTED** to **BEAT** the **ODDS** (and how **YOU** can too)

By Karen & Chad Lilly

**BEHRMAN HOUSE**
www.behrmanhouse.com

For our beautiful kids, Cameron and Bryn, who inspire us to keep growing and learning. Thank you. We love you!!—KL and CL

Published by Behrman House, Millburn, New Jersey 07041
www.behrmanhouse.com

Text copyright © 2020 by Karen and Chad Lilly
ISBN 978-0-87441-977-1

Design by Terry Taylor Studio
Edited by Ann D. Koffsky

Library of Congress Cataloging-in-Publication Data

Names: Lilly, Karen, author. | Lilly, Chad, author. | Koffsky, Ann D., editor.
Title: The failure book / by Karen and Chad Lilly ; edited by Ann D. Koffsky.
Description: Millburn, New Jersey : Behrman House, [2020] | Audience:
  Grades: 4-6 | Summary: "What do Albert Einstein, Michael Jordan, JK
  Rowling, P!nk, and Abraham Lincoln all have in common? They messed up.
  They miscalculated. They made mistakes. They FAILED. So did every one of
  the extraordinary people profiled. One couldn't get into college and
  another lost several elections. One was sent to prison and another had
  his factory blow up. Yet when faced with failure, each found ways to
  persist, beat the odds, and come out on top" -- Provided by publisher.
Identifiers: LCCN 2019033043 | ISBN 9780874419771 (trade paperback)
Subjects: LCSH: Celebrities--Biography--Juvenile literature. | Successful
  people--Biography--Juvenile literature. | Failure (Psychology)--Juvenile
  literature. | Success--Juvenile literature. | Persistence--Juvenile
  literature.
Classification: LCC CT107 .L55 2019 | DDC 920.02--dc23
LC record available at https://lccn.loc.gov/2019033043

Printed in the United States of America

1 3 5 7 9 8 6 4 2

# Table of Contents

# Everybody Fails

Have you ever tried out for a team—and not made it? Totally bombed on a test? Sung your heart out at an audition, hoping to get the starring role, and then got offered a minor part in the chorus or no part at all? Have you ever FAILED?

Of course you have—we all have. Even brilliant people like Albert Einstein and J. K. Rowling have struggled to overcome failure. In this book, you'll read about how they and twenty other incredibly successful people accomplished their dreams and changed the world for the better, all while overcoming their own failures.

What would the world be like today had they not persevered and risen above their challenges? How did they do it? They had resilience. They were comfortable with being uncomfortable. No matter how many times they fell down, they would always get back up again—just like you did as a baby learning to walk. What would happen if we could all recapture this resilience and pursue our goals with that same fearless enthusiasm?

Think of this book as a game. Start by guessing who each person is as you read about their failures. Then turn the page to discover who the mystery person is, and find out more about them.

At the end of each chapter, complete the challenges. They'll help you think about how to accomplish your own goals, achieve success, and overcome any bumps and obstacles you may encounter along the way.

# Chapter 1
## Scientists

# he Physicist:
# Who Am I?

I didn't speak until I was four years old.

I was told by one of my teachers that I would never amount to anything.

After graduating from college, I couldn't find a job in my field.

I didn't learn to read until I was over seven years old.

I was expelled from elementary school and called a "lazy dog" and a "bad influence on my classmates."

I failed the entrance exam to Zurich Polytechnic, a university focused on science and engineering.

My first published scientific paper was largely ignored.

# Albert Einstein
## (1879 – 1955)

> "It's not that I'm so smart, it's just that I stay with problems longer."

One of the highest compliments you can receive is being called an "Einstein." Albert Einstein made such significant contributions to the world of science and physics that his name has become synonymous with outstanding intelligence. He came up with revolutionary ideas and equations that changed people's view of the world and contributed to modern-day tools such as GPS and digital cameras. Einstein also spoke out against injustice and tried to help others.

> "The true sign of intelligence is not knowledge but imagination."

- ◆ Albert Einstein won the Nobel Prize in 1921 and developed revolutionary scientific theories, including the theory of relativity, which is expressed mathematically as $E=mc^2$.

- ◆ He was named "Person of the Century" by *Time Magazine* in 1999.

- ◆ Einstein was one of four people who signed a peace manifesto in 1914 protesting Germany's military aggression; later he risked his life and spoke out against the Nazis while he lived in Germany.

- ◆ He was known for helping children in his neighborhood with their math homework and sharing his lunch with them.

$$E=mc^2$$

> "Anyone who has never made a mistake has never tried anything new."

# The Chemist:
## Who Am I?

I had many lab accidents, and many of my experiments failed.

I was refused membership in the French Academy of Sciences.

I was not admitted to university in my home country of Poland, so I moved to France to get a college education.

Because I didn't know French when I began school, I often didn't understand my professors and struggled to be as prepared as my French counterparts.

After completing my degree in chemistry, I returned home to Poland hoping to find work in a lab, but I failed to get a job.

# Marie Curie
## (1867 – 1934)

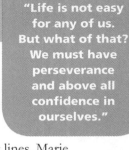

"Life is not easy for any of us. But what of that? We must have perseverance and above all confidence in ourselves."

Whether she was moving to a new country to get an education, discovering two previously unknown chemical elements, or learning auto-mechanic skills in order to drive her mobile X-ray vehicles to the front lines, Marie Curie was the embodiment of adaptability and persistence. Rather than let obstacles stop her, she found ways to work around them and get things done.

"I was taught that the way of progress was neither swift nor easy."

- Marie Curie was the first woman to win a Nobel Prize, and the first person in history to win two Nobel Prizes (in Physics in 1903 and Chemistry in 1911).

- She was the first woman in France to earn a doctorate in science and the first female professor at the University of Paris, also known as the Sorbonne.

- Curie created mobile X-ray vehicles, nicknamed "little Curies," to help treat injured soldiers.

- It is estimated that her X-ray equipment and the radon gas syringe she designed to sterilize wounds may have saved the lives of one million soldiers.

- Curie, and her husband, Pierre, discovered two chemical elements, polonium and radium, and did pioneering work in radioactivity.

"One never notices what has been done; one can only see what remains to be done."

# The Inventor:
## Who Am I?

I was fired from my first two jobs for being unproductive.

Some of my teachers told me that I was too stupid to learn anything.

My first patent was for an automatic vote recorder, which I failed to sell.

I failed hundreds of times before I was able to make my most famous invention work.

When I was a child, I made a science lab while on a train, causing the baggage compartment to catch fire.

I invented a talking doll, but customers complained that it broke too easily and had a terrible voice. It went off the market a few weeks after it was sent to stores.

# Thomas Edison
## (1847 – 1931)

Platinum, hickory, and cedar are just a few of the many materials Thomas Edison tried to use as lightbulb filaments, only to watch them fail. Many people would have given up in frustration, but not Edison. He kept experimenting, and over the course of his lifetime was issued more than a thousand patents for his inventions, the world record at the time.

"Genius is 1 percent inspiration and 99 percent perspiration."

"When you have exhausted all possibilities, remember this— you haven't."

- ◆ Thomas Edison invented the electric light bulb, as well as lamps to put them in, switches to turn them on and off, and electric wiring for people's homes.

- ◆ He was cofounder of the General Electric power company, which today makes a wide range of products, including turbines, jet engines, and medical devices.

- ◆ Edison helped the US Navy do research to prepare for World War I.

- ◆ He helped start a government research lab, which led to many inventions, including radar, jet engines, and the internet.

- ◆ He was given a Congressional Gold Medal in 1928.

- ◆ In 1996 *Life Magazine* named Edison the "Man of the Millennium."

Think about a problem that you are struggling with in your life. Define it in the inner circle (sometimes just clearly defining a problem helps you find a solution).

Write your problem here.

What are new ways to solve the problem? Write one in each arrow.

# Chapter 2
## Advocates

# The Activist: Who Am I?

I became a lawyer, and at my first trial I was tongue-tied and did such a terrible job that I decided to return the fee that my client had paid me.

I didn't get good grades in elementary school.

I was arrested and sent to prison many times. I started referring to prison as "His Majesty's Hotels," and used my time there to catch up on my reading.

I didn't know how to use a knife or fork and couldn't speak English well when I first arrived in England.

My law practice went out of business after just two years.

I was accused of being a traitor and beaten up by some of my own supporters.

# Mahatma Gandhi
## (1869 – 1948)

> "Freedom is not worth having if it does not include the freedom to make mistakes."

At five feet five, 102 pounds, and wearing the humble clothing of the poor, the gentle Mahatma Gandhi was an unlikely candidate to lead an independence movement. But that's exactly what he did. Using peaceful tactics, Gandhi and his followers achieved independence for India from the British Empire. Their success proved that nonviolent strategies can lead to victory.

> "Be the change that you wish to see in the world."

- Gandhi believed that all human beings are equal, and spent a lifetime teaching that idea and working toward making it a reality.

- He took a twelve-thousand-mile pilgrimage across India to meet people and encourage them to give up their prejudices toward those at the bottom of society, called "untouchables."

- Gandhi's message of nonviolence and love influenced leaders around the world, including Martin Luther King Jr. and the Dalai Lama.

> "Live as if you were to die tomorrow. Learn as if you were to live forever."

# The Preacher:
## Who Am I?

I got a C in public speaking at seminary.

I led a campaign to desegregate public parks in Georgia. It was unsuccessful.

When a protest march that I was organizing was met with a legal challenge, many of my supporters decided not to participate.

I was arrested for holding peaceful boycotts.

I tried to register African-American voters in the South, but many of my supporters were assaulted, and I was able to register only two thousand people.

Many of my own supporters questioned the effectiveness of my methods.

# Martin Luther King Jr.
## (1929 – 1968)

He was vilified. Physically attacked. Imprisoned. Targeted by the FBI. He was called a traitor, and the majority of Americans disapproved of him. Despite this, Martin Luther King Jr. continued to fight for equality. Today, he is remembered for his work fighting for a more just society, and a federal holiday is named in his honor.

"Faith is taking the first step even when you don't see the whole staircase."

◆ King's work led to the passage of the Civil Rights Act in 1964 and the Voting Rights Act in 1965.

◆ He won the Nobel Peace Prize in 1964.

◆ King was a master orator and gave many inspiring speeches. He delivered his most famous speech, "I Have a Dream," in 1963 at the March on Washington for Jobs and Freedom.

◆ After being attacked on stage by an audience member, King, bleeding, asked his supporters to pray for his attacker and not hurt him.

"We must accept finite disappointment, but never lose infinite hope."

"Darkness cannot drive out darkness; only light can do that. Hate cannot drive out hate; only love can do that."

# The Environmentalist: Who Am I?

I ran for a seat in parliament and lost.

A tree nursery I started failed because of a drought. Almost all of the seedlings died.

I tried to start a union to help women get equal rights, but the courts refused to allow it.

When I arrived to start my new job, I was informed that I had lost the position to someone else.

I ran for president and lost.

I was sent to prison repeatedly for being outspoken and leading peaceful protests in support of the environment.

I was denounced as a traitor and a rebel in my country.

# WANGARI MAATHAI
## (1940 – 2011)

"Remember what millions of hands can do," said Wangari Maathai. She started an environmental movement by planting a single tree. From there Maathai went on to found the Green Belt Movement in Kenya, which has planted over fifty-one million trees and trained over thirty thousand women in forestry and beekeeping since 1977. Maathai's work continues to inspire people from across the planet to value and take care of nature.

"It's the little things citizens do. That's what will make the difference. My little thing is planting trees."

◆ In 2004, Wangari Maathai became the first African woman to receive the Nobel Peace Prize.

◆ Maathai inspired and led the launch of the United Nations' billion tree campaign, which has planted over twelve billion trees across the planet.

◆ She was the first woman in East or Central Africa to earn a doctorate.

◆ Maathai was a member of Kenya's parliament and the assistant minister for the environment and natural resources.

◆ She founded the Institute for Peace & Environmental Studies at the University of Nairobi.

"There are opportunities even in the most difficult moments."

"I have seen rivers...become clean-flowing again...The job is hardly over, but it no longer seems impossible."

# The Nurse:
# Who Am I?

I didn't get the job of principal at the school that I founded.

As a child I had a lisp and was teased often. I didn't have many friends.

I wanted to go onto battlefields to help wounded soldiers, but I couldn't get a permit. I went anyway.

I was demoted from my job in the US patent office.

I was investigated by the Senate for misusing money. Eventually, I was cleared of wrongdoing, but my reputation was damaged.

Even though it was eventually signed, I tried and failed for years to get the U.S. government to sign the Geneva Convention, which helps ensure that captured soldiers receive humane treatment during wartime.

# Clara Barton
## (1821 – 1912)

In the midst of a raging Civil War battle, filled with cannon fire, smoke, and bullets whizzing through the air, Clara Barton risked her life to give medical care to injured soldiers on the battlefield. Throughout her lifetime, Barton was a champion for soldiers, women, African Americans, and all people who faced suffering.

"The door that nobody else will go in seems always to swing widely open for me."

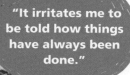

"It irritates me to be told how things have always been done."

- Clara Barton founded the American Red Cross and served as its president. Today, the American Red Cross helps millions of people around the world.

- She created the first free public school in New Jersey.

- Barton, a teacher, was inspired to help her former students fighting in the Civil War. She used her own money and collected donations from around the country to purchase and bring supplies to the front lines.

- She braved the battlefield when few others would and gave soldiers water, food, and medical care, regardless of which side they fought for, Union or Confederate.

- Barton was known by the nickname "Angel of the Battlefield."

UNITED STATES POSTAGE
FOUNDER OF THE
3¢
CLARA BARTON
AMERICAN RED CROSS

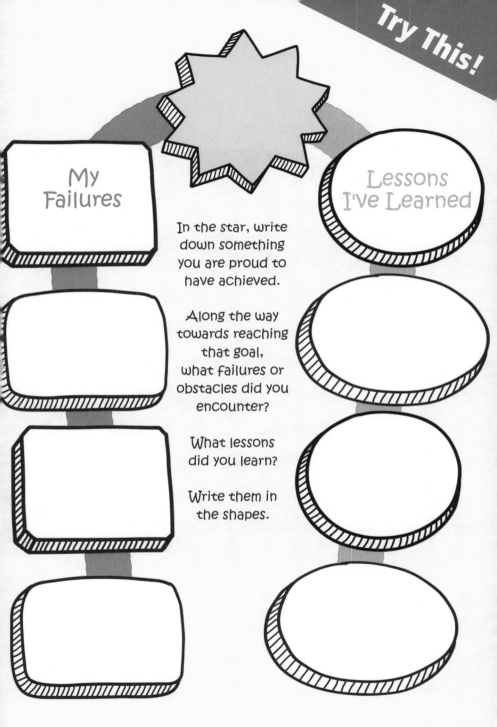

My
Failures

Lessons
I've Learned

In the star, write
down something
you are proud to
have achieved.

Along the way
towards reaching
that goal,
what failures or
obstacles did you
encounter?

What lessons
did you learn?

Write them in
the shapes.

23

# Chapter 3
## National Leaders

# The Uniter:
# Who Am I?

I never went to college and barely had any formal education.

I came up with the idea for a device that would help ships avoid getting stuck on sandbars, got a patent for it, but wasn't able to manufacture it.

I ran for a position in my state's legislature and lost.

I ran for Speaker of the House of Representatives in my state and lost.

A newspaper once described me as "...weak, wishy-washy" and "a laughing-stock of the whole world."

I ran for the Senate and lost. Twice.

I ran for vice president of the United States and lost.

# Abraham Lincoln
## (1809 – 1865)

> "Most folks are as happy as they make up their minds to be."

Using about 270 words, Abraham Lincoln delivered a speech that changed the course of US history: the Gettysburg Address. With that speech, he displayed the profound wisdom, compassion, and leadership that allowed him to skillfully steer the United States away from slavery and closer to the ideals of freedom and equality for all.

> "I say 'try'—if we never try, we shall never succeed."

- ◆ Abraham Lincoln was the sixteenth president of the United States and is widely considered to be one of the greatest presidents in US history.

- ◆ Despite being hated by people on both sides for not doing enough to eliminate slavery or for doing too much, Lincoln stayed firm in his convictions.

- ◆ He led the Union to victory over the Confederacy in the Civil War and preserved the United States of America.

- ◆ Lincoln issued the Emancipation Proclamation, which led to the Thirteenth Amendment, formally ending slavery in the United States.

> "Do I not destroy my enemies when I make them my friends?"

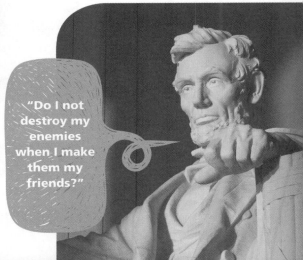

# The War Hero:
## Who Am I?

I failed the entrance test for military college. Twice.

I was not a high-achieving student in school and couldn't speak clearly.

My first campaign for a seat in the House of Commons failed.

"Address, accent, appearance do not help him," is how a newspaper reporter described me.

I proposed marriage to four women. Three rejected me.

Even though I led my country to victory against an evil tyrant, I was still voted out of office.

# Winston Churchill
## (1874 – 1965)

When Nazi bombs rained down on London during World War II, they left the shattered city in heaps of rubble. The spirit of the British people, however, stayed strong, due in large part to one man: Winston Churchill. With his masterful oratory skills, unfaltering conviction, and staunch leadership, Churchill inspired the British people to continue fighting even in the face of overwhelming odds, and ultimately led them to victory.

"Success is going from failure to failure without loss of enthusiasm."

- ◆ Winston Churchill served as the prime minister of Great Britain twice, from 1940 to 1945 and 1951 to 1955.

- ◆ He led England when it was the only nation in Europe taking a stand against Hitler, the Nazis, and Germany.

- ◆ Churchill chose to stay in London during the Nazi bombings, demonstrating that he was willing to make any sacrifice for Britain and its people.

- ◆ Churchill was knighted by Queen Elizabeth II in 1953.

- ◆ He was awarded the Nobel Prize in Literature in 1953 for "mastery of historical and biographical description as well as for brilliant oratory in defending exalted human values."

"Success is not final, failure is not fatal: It is the courage to continue that counts."

28

# The Revolutionary:
## Who Am I?

I lost many more battles than I won.

I lost a battle in the French and Indian War and was forced to surrender. I was demoted when I returned home.

I was a terrible speller.

I was not a great public speaker.

I was called a "fake patriot" and a "hypocrite" in a newspaper article.

I was turned down multiple times when I tried to become an officer and failed to fulfill my dream of having a career in the British Royal Army.

# George Washington
## (1732 – 1799)

Suffering from bitter cold, food shortages, and a lack of other basic supplies, General George Washington and his soldiers endured severe hardship during the Revolutionary War. Yet, against incredible odds, Washington led his ill-equipped, half-starved army to victory over Great Britain, the most powerful military of the time. His extraordinary leadership and integrity continued through his presidency and led the American people to refer affectionately to him as the "father of our country."

"Perseverance and spirit have done wonders in all ages."

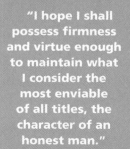

- George Washington was the first president of the United States.

- King George III of England said that if Washington chose to give up power, which he did, "he would be the greatest man on earth."

- Washington chose to serve only two terms, setting the precedent that American presidents would not serve for more than two terms.

- Today, the president of the United States is still simply called "Mr. President," a tradition established by Washington. He rejected all other suggestions, including "His Elective Highness," "Majesty," and "His Mightiness."

"The harder the conflict, the greater the triumph."

"I hope I shall possess firmness and virtue enough to maintain what I consider the most enviable of all titles, the character of an honest man."

**STEP 1:**

On a scale of 1-10, how happy do you feel right now?
Circle the number on the scale.

**STEP 2:**

List five things you are grateful for:

1. _____

2. _____

3. _____

4. _____

5. _____

**STEP 3:**

After listing these things, NOW how happy do you feel?

**STEP 4:**

Think about: Did you feel happier or less happy after completing the list?
How can working on your mood help you handle challenges that come
your way?

# Chapter 4
## Business Leaders

# The Investor:
## Who Am I?

I was rejected by Harvard Business School.

I offered to work for my mentor for free, and I still didn't get the job.

I bought several businesses that failed.

People on Wall Street accused me of getting my ideas from tipsters rather than giving me credit for my own painstaking research.

I was belittled and ignored by scholars in my field. One noted economist attributed my success to Nebraska insurance law, not my skills.

At one point, I lost over half of my money in the stock market.

# Warren Buffett
## (born 1930)

Known as the "Oracle of Omaha," Warren Buffett made his fortune by bucking trends. He did not believe in making a profit at any cost. Buffett valued integrity and honesty, even above making money, and is quoted as saying: "If you lose money for the firm I will be understanding. If you lose reputation, I will be ruthless." Over time, Buffett's strategy of staying true to his principles paid off, and in 2008 he became the wealthiest person on the planet and continues to be among the top ten.

"The best thing I did was choose the right heroes."

- ◆ Warren Buffett is considered to be one of the greatest investors of all time.

- ◆ Buffett has committed to giving an estimated $40 billion to charity over several years.

- ◆ He has inspired other wealthy individuals to give generously as well.

- ◆ Buffett received the Presidential Medal of Freedom in 2011, the highest civilian honor given by the US government.

- ◆ Despite his wealth, Buffett lives modestly in the same house he bought in Omaha, Nebraska, in 1958 for $31,500.

"I don't look to jump over seven-foot bars; I look around for one-foot bars that I can step over."

Buffett's hom

# The Entrepreneur:
## Who Am I?

I had a C average in high school.

I was rejected by the Officer Candidate School of the Armed Forces.

I was fired from my job at a brokerage firm.

My public speaking style was described as a "nasal, uninspired monotone."

I tried and failed to bring the Olympics to my city.

Media experts thought that I would be crushed when I ran for mayor.

I tried and failed to get a new stadium and convention center built in my city.

# Michael Bloomberg
## (born 1942)

The day after Michael Bloomberg was fired from his job at an investment bank, he started his own company, Bloomberg L.P. The business was an enormous success and made Bloomberg a billionaire. Following that success, he went on to be elected mayor of New York City three times, and later ran for president. He applied his business know-how to governing, and the initiatives he implemented as mayor are today used as models for cities around the world.

"Life is too short to spend your time avoiding failure."

- ◆ Michael Bloomberg invented the "Bloomberg terminal" and its accompanying software system, which helps people who work in finance analyze securities and stocks.

- ◆ The memory of his hardworking but low-paid father writing a check for twenty-five dollars to charity inspired him to found Bloomberg Philanthropies, which supports public health, arts and culture, the environment, education, and government innovation.

- ◆ As mayor, Bloomberg erased New York City's budget deficit, banned smoking in public spaces, added bike lanes and parks, and helped make the city safer.

"You must first be willing to fail—and you must have the courage to go for it anyway."

"If you don't encounter setbacks in your career, if you don't have doubts...you're not dreaming big enough."

# The Mechanic:
## Who Am I?

I dropped out of school at age fifteen.

I worked for years designing a new piston ring for cars and tried to sell it to a major motor company, but they rejected it.

I went back to school with the hope of improving my piston ring, but engineers at my school laughed at my designs.

I built a factory, but it was bombed and destroyed in World War II.

I used gasoline cans as raw material to rebuild my factory, but it was demolished by an earthquake soon after I rebuilt it.

I created an automotive-parts company in 1937, but because people couldn't afford to buy new cars at the time, it failed.

# Soichiro Honda
## (1906 – 1991)

"Don't touch the cars! Your job is to sweep my garage and clean the tools, nothing else!" yelled the boss to a young Soichiro Honda. Poor and uneducated, Honda was treated terribly at his job, but he didn't let that deter him from his love of automobiles. Much later, as an adult, Honda created his own car company, where he chose to show his employees respect and appreciation.

"Success represents the one percent of your work which results from the 99 percent that is called failure."

- Soichiro Honda founded the Honda Motor Company, which today is a multibillion-dollar company that employs over two hundred thousand people worldwide.

- He received the highest honor given by Japan's emperor, the Order of the Sacred Treasure, first class, and was inducted into the Automotive Hall of Fame.

- Honda listened to and considered his employees' ideas. Often he would implement those ideas and give the employees credit.

- Today, the Honda Motor Company develops fuel-efficient, reliable vehicles that continue to be among the world's top sellers.

"Success can only be achieved through repeated failures and introspection."

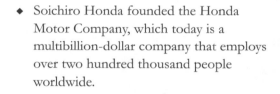

Complete your "HERO TREE."

On each branch, write the name of one of your heroes. In the leaves, jot down what you admire about each of those heroes.

Got more heroes? Add more branches and leaves to your tree.

Your name here

39

# Chapter 5
## Athletes

# The Basketball Player:
## Who Am I?

When I played minor league baseball, I would start practicing my swing at 7:30 a.m. and keep going until my hands bled. But I still achieved only a .202 career batting average.

I couldn't get a date in high school.

After failing to make the varsity basketball team in high school, I went to my room, closed the door, and couldn't stop crying.

I missed more than nine thousand basketball shots in my career.

I lost almost three hundred games in my career.

I missed the game-winning shot twenty-six times in my career.

# Michael Jordan
## (born 1963)

Michael Jordan elevated the popularity of the NBA by showing the world moves never seen before. Whether launching from the free throw line or leaping past seven-foot-tall players to dunk the basketball, he seemed to fly on the court, floating above the game as if suspended on wires. He may not have been the tallest or strongest NBA player ever, but his exceptional commitment, work ethic, and skills were unrivaled.

"I've failed over and over and over again in my life. And that is why I succeed."

- ◆ Michael Jordan is considered by many to be the greatest basketball player of all time because of his exceptional skills on both offense and defense.

- ◆ He is a six-time NBA champion, a five-time NBA MVP, a ten-time scoring champion, a nine-time All-Defensive First Team, and a two-time Gold Medal Olympian.

- ◆ Jordan was inducted into the Naismith Memorial Basketball Hall of Fame in 2009.

- ◆ He is the first-ever former player to become CEO and primary owner of an NBA franchise, the Charlotte Hornets.

"You must expect great things of yourself before you can do them."

# The Swimmer:
## Who Am I?

I failed to qualify for the Olympics in the 50-meter freestyle, which I was favored to win.

I was kicked off my training team.

Even though I was ranked number one in the world when I entered an Olympic finals, I failed to get a medal and instead came in seventh overall.

I lost a race because I kept watching my competitors instead of staying focused on my own performance.

I failed to make the Olympic swim team by just 0.09 seconds.

I tried to train with an elite coach, but he rejected me.

# DARA TORRES
## (born 1967)

Take your mark….BEEP! Dara Torres launched into the water, sped to the other side of the Olympic-sized pool, and broke her first world record at age fifteen. Twenty-six years later, at age forty-one, Torres propelled herself into the record books again, breaking the American record in the 50-meter freestyle. With endurance and grit, Torres has become an icon in the swimming world, inspiring many to never give up no matter their age.

"Never worry about what anyone else is doing... Just swim your race."

- ◆ Dara Torres broke six different world records across three different events.

- ◆ She won twenty-eight NCAA All-American swimming honors during her career at the University of Florida, which is the most an athlete can earn in that sport.

- ◆ With twelve medals, Torres has tied for the most decorated female swimmer in Olympic history.

- ◆ She was inducted into the International Jewish Sports Hall of Fame in 2005.

- ◆ Torres swam in her fifth Olympic Games at the age of forty-one, earning her the honor of being the oldest US Olympic swimmer in history.

- ◆ She was the first American swimmer to appear in five Olympics.

"The water doesn't know how old you are."

# The Tennis Player:
## Who Am I?

I lost my first two professional tournaments, in the first round.

I lost my first Grand Slam tournament.

At one of my tournaments, the crowd booed and screamed insults at me.

My ranking fell from number 1 in the world to number 139.

In one tournament, I wasn't considered good enough to be ranked at all.

A national newspaper said I would never amount to anything compared to my sister.

# SERENA WILLIAMS
## (born 1981)

No one in the world has revolutionized women's tennis more than Serena Williams. From her incredible strength and athleticism, to her cutting-edge fashion on the court (including a tutu and a catsuit!), Williams has helped transform the image of tennis from a privileged, largely homogeneous sport to a more modern, diverse, and intense one. She is a superstar tennis player and is considered one of the greatest athletes of all time.

"I don't like to lose— at anything...Yet I've grown most not from victories, but setbacks."

◆ Serena Williams has won more tennis titles than any other professional tennis player, male or female.

◆ She was the first solo black woman to be named *Sports Illustrated*'s "Sportsperson of the Year."

◆ Williams is a four-time Olympic gold medalist.

◆ As a child, Williams was unable to afford tennis lessons, club fees, or even a junior tennis racket. She practiced on a cracked, littered tennis court in her neighborhood of Compton, California.

◆ As a UNICEF Goodwill Ambassador, she focused on education for vulnerable children in Africa and Asia.

"Since I don't look like every other girl, it takes a while to be okay with that. To be different. But different is good."

"I really think a champion is defined not by their wins but by how they can recover when they fall."

What is one goal you want to achieve this year? Write it on the backboard.

In each basketball, starting from the lowest one, write down one simple habit (an action you do regularly) to get you a little closer to your goal.

# Chapter 6
## Artists

# The Actor:
# Who Am I?

I failed to get the role as "first gravedigger" in my high school production of *Hamlet*.

**I wasn't able to get a date to my high school dances.**

**I wanted to be a pilot but was rejected from flight school.**

I was kicked off my college football team because I got arrested for having a fight.

I couldn't support myself through acting, so I worked odd jobs selling encyclopedias door-to-door, working on a farm, and digging balls out of the mud at a golf course.

I auditioned for a movie and didn't get the role. My friend got the part instead.

**My first movie was described as "static and disappointing" by the *New York Daily News*. When it later aired on TV, I bought newspaper ads apologizing for my performance.**

My television series was cancelled after only four months.

# PAUL NEWMAN
## (1925 – 2008)

"Sometimes God makes perfect people, and Paul Newman was one of them," remarked fellow Oscar winner Sally Field. Newman became world-famous as a Hollywood superstar, and followed that with a second career as an entrepreneur and philanthropist. Whether he was sneaking hundreds of live chickens into a director's trailer as a prank or stirring the first batch of his Newman's Own salad dressing with a canoe paddle in his barn, Paul Newman did things his way, with humor, originality, and generosity.

"I don't think there's anything exceptional or noble in being philanthropic. It's the other attitudes that confuse me."

- Paul Newman acted in over fifty movies.

- He was nominated for an Academy Award ten times and won the Oscar for Best Actor in 1987 for his role in *The Color of Money*.

- He cofounded Newman's Own, a food company that gives 100 percent of its profits to charity. Newman joked that he was embarrassed to see his salad dressing make more money than his movies.

- Newman described his proudest achievement as creating the "Hole in the Wall Gang," a camp for children with cancer.

- He received a Kennedy Center Honors award in 1992, and the Jean Hersholt Humanitarian Award in 1993 for his philanthropic work.

"A man can only be judged by his actions, and not by his good intentions or his beliefs."

# The Actress:
# Who Am I?

I felt ugly compared to other girls.

My dream to be a ballerina was shattered when I wasn't chosen to go on tour with my dance company.

I was turned down for my first Hollywood movie role.

I starred in a movie that critics described as "witless, contrived, and pointless."

I lost the role of Cleopatra to another actress, who was paid $1 million, an unprecedented amount of money for a female actress.

I was told by a producer that I was too fat to be in his show.

# Audrey Hepburn
## (1929 – 1993)

> "For beautiful eyes, look for the good in others; for beautiful lips, speak only words of kindness...."

Audrey Hepburn was the Hollywood superstar known for wearing a tiara, a little black dress, and pearls. Her great beauty and sense of style made her a fashion icon, and her signature look still influences designers and image makers today. She is one of only fourteen people who have won an Emmy, Grammy, Oscar, and Tony award, known as an EGOT.

> "There is no deficit in human resources. There is only a deficit in human will."

> "I believe in being strong when everything seems to be going wrong."

- ◆ Audrey Hepburn was nominated for a Best Actress Academy Award four times and won for her role in *Roman Holiday*.

- ◆ During World War II, she was a teenager living in Holland and performed in illegal, secret recitals there to help raise money for those fighting the Nazis. She also risked her life helping allied airmen escape Nazi capture.

- ◆ Through her work as Goodwill Ambassador for UNICEF, Hepburn helped poverty-stricken children in war-ridden nations around the world.

- ◆ She received the Presidential Medal of Freedom in 1992 and was posthumously awarded the Jean Hersholt Humanitarian Award in recognition of her work on behalf of suffering children around the world.

# The Author: Who Am I?

**Publishers rejected my first book twelve times.**

A publisher advised me to get a day job because I would not make money writing children's books.

I lost my job as a secretary when I was caught writing stories at work.

Because I couldn't afford decent housing, I had to live in an apartment infested with mice.

I moved out of the country to focus on writing my book but failed to make progress. When I came back home, I had no finished book, no job, and a failed marriage.

I was rejected by my first-choice college, Oxford University.

# J. K. Rowling
## (born 1965)

Sitting and writing in a coffee shop in England, an unemployed, single mother living on welfare created the world of Harry Potter. With exotic creatures, endearing characters, heroic adventure, and epic battles between good and evil, J. K. Rowling captured the attention of millions of fans of all ages. Rowling, now one of the bestselling authors of all time, has lived the ultimate rags-to-riches success story and has shown the importance of persistence.

"Anything is possible if you have enough nerve."

- J. K. Rowling has sold over half a billion books worldwide, in two hundred countries.

- Her books have been translated into eighty languages.

- Rowling's Harry Potter books have been made into successful movies and are the inspiration for Harry Potter theme parks.

- She lost her status as the world's first female billionaire novelist after giving an estimated $160 million to charity.

"We do not need magic to transform our world. We carry all of the power we need inside ourselves already."

# The Director:
## Who Am I?

I dropped out of college.

Professionals in the movie business told me that my work wasn't worth watching.

I was rejected by two film schools.

My first movie had disappointing ticket sales.

My actors threatened to go on strike because my movie took too long to make.

Even after I spent $700,000 to design an alien character for one of my movies, it still failed to look the way I needed it to.

# Steven Spielberg
## (born 1946)

Indiana Jones races toward the exit as a giant boulder rolls after him in *Raiders of the Lost Ark*, menacing dinosaurs are resurrected in *Jurassic Park*, bullets rip along the beaches of Normandy on D-Day in *Saving Private Ryan*, and a terrifying shark comes to life in *Jaws*. With these and many other powerful scenes, Steven Spielberg defined himself as one of the most brilliant and successful directors of all time.

"All good ideas start out as bad ideas, that's why it takes so long."

◆ Steven Spielberg has received two Oscars for Best Director and one for Best Picture.

◆ The massive success of *Jaws* led many to describe Spielberg as the inventor of the summer blockbuster movie.

◆ He has worked on over one hundred projects for TV and film.

◆ To date, his films have produced the highest worldwide box office results of any director.

◆ Spielberg's meetings with Holocaust survivors during the production of his movie *Schindler's List* inspired him to establish the USC Shoah Foundation, which interviews Holocaust survivors and records their stories.

"Failure is inevitable. Success is elusive."

# The Singer: Who Am I?

When I was a child, I wasn't allowed to visit my friends because their parents thought I was a bad influence.

I broke the law as a teenager. I smoked, drank, and used and sold drugs.

I was arrested for petty theft and trespassing.

I dropped out of high school at age fifteen.

I was kicked out of my house by my mom when I was fifteen because of my rebellious lifestyle.

The first singing group I joined fell apart. The next group I joined also broke up.

# P!NK Alecia Beth Moore (born 1979)

Suspended upside-down from the ceiling by ribbons during a Grammy performance, P!nk once again showed her fans why she is such an enduring rock star. Despite being criticized for everything from being too old to too edgy to too outspoken, P!nk continues to stay true to herself. For her, this was a successful strategy and allowed her to go from working at McDonald's to becoming a world-famous performer.

"You can't move mountains by whispering at them."

- ◆ P!nk has sold over seventy-five million singles and forty million albums worldwide.

- ◆ She has been awarded three Grammys, a Daytime Emmy, and seven MTV Video Music Awards.

- ◆ Billboard, which tracks the most popular songs and albums, named P!nk the "Pop Songs Artist of the Decade" in 2009 and "Woman of the Year" in 2013.

- ◆ She is a vocal advocate for the LGBTQ community, supports organizations such as People for the Ethical Treatment of Animals and Save the Children, and is a UNICEF Ambassador.

"Embrace the freak that you are."

# The Chef:
## Who Am I?

I wanted to work at the *New Yorker* magazine, but I couldn't even get an interview there.

I flunked the entry-level typing test at *Newsweek* magazine.

I failed part of my final exam at Le Cordon Bleu culinary school in Paris.

I tried to get my recipes published in magazines, but they were all rejected.

I was fired from my job as an advertising manager.

My publisher rejected the first draft of my cookbook. I worked on the second draft for years, and then my publisher rejected that too.

Because I made lots of mistakes on my televised cooking show, critics often described me as a clown.

# Julia Child
## (1912 – 2004)

Whether she was live on late-night TV making an appetizer of raw beef instead of a hamburger because the stove didn't work, or losing track of where she'd placed a casserole, Julia Child responded to those inevitable cooking disasters with charm and wit. One of the original celebrity chefs, she was adored by millions for her culinary skill, humor, and willingness to show her goofy imperfections.

"The only real stumbling block is fear of failure."

"The only way you learn how to flip things is just to flip them."

- On her TV show *The French Chef*, and in her cookbook *Mastering the Art of French Cooking*, Julia Child helped America's home cooks move away from heating up frozen dinners to experimenting with sophisticated gourmet meals.

- She received a Primetime Emmy award and numerous honorary doctorates.

- Child was the first woman inducted into the Culinary Institute of America's Hall of Fame in 1993.

- She was awarded France's highest decoration, the National Order of the Legion of Honour, in 2000, and the United States' highest civilian honor, the Presidential Medal of Freedom, in 2003.

- Child established the "Julia Child Foundation for Gastronomy and the Culinary Arts," which supports scholarships and food literacy programs.

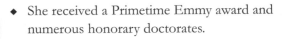

Fill this page with words and pictures that show a part of your personality. Write words that are a **BIG** part of you large, and those that describe a TINY part of you small.

Tape a picture of you
**HERE**

# KEEP GROWING!

Can you imagine what the world would be like today if the twenty-two people you just read about had given up after their first, second, or third failure? Or worse, if they had doubted their abilities and never even tried? We would not have the United States of America as we know it, the light bulb, the American Red Cross, and so much more.

The people in this book each imagined the seemingly impossible and then made it happen. They chose not to give up, no matter how many obstacles they encountered or how great their struggles.

What will the world gain if you pursue your dreams, whatever they may be, however big or small? If you're able to embrace difficulties as they unfold, learn from them, and have faith in yourself, nothing can stop you.

**"Never, never, never give up."**
**—Winston Churchill**

*"No one is born a great cook, one learns by doing."*
—Julia Child

"There are only two ways to live your life. One is as though nothing is a miracle. The other is as though everything is a miracle."
— Albert Einstein

"Never put an age limit on your dreams."
—Dara Torres

"I can accept failure, everyone fails at something. But I can't accept not trying." —Michael Jordan

"Love is the only force capable of transforming an enemy into a friend."
—Martin Luther King Jr.

"Whenever you have truth it must be given with love, or the message and the messenger will be rejected."
— Mahatma Gandhi

"I am a slow walker, but I never walk backwards."
—Abraham Lincoln

"Many of life's failures are people who did not realize how close they were to success when they gave up."— Thomas Edison

"Chains of habit are too light to be felt until they are too heavy to be broken."
—Warren Buffett

# Quotes that Inspire Me

Photo credits: The publisher gratefully acknowledges the following sources of images:
(L=Left; R=Right) Wikimedia Commons: Cover; 1T; 8R; 10L; 18R; 22L; 28L; 34R; 44; 50; 52L; 60R. The Asahi Shimbun via Getty Images 38L. Shutterstock: Sylverarts Vectors and Sapunkele (bkgrnds); Andrei Verner 8 (illios); vkilikov 10R; Everett Historical 12L; samnit 12R; topform 13; StockImageFactory.com 16R; d_odin 16L; Uncle Leo 18L; s_bukley 20; chrisdorney 22R; Everett Historical 26L, 30; Kent Weakley 26R; Olga Popova 28R, 60L; EniaB 31; 360b 36; Kent Sievers 34L; otomobil 38R; Ihnatovich Maryia 39; Natasha Pankina 42R,47; landmarkmedia 42L; Jimmie48 Photography 46; Everett Collection 54; Anton_Ivanov 52R; taniavolobueva 56L; otted Yeti 56R; Tinseltown 58L; J.A. Dunbar 58R.